# CONTENTS

# THE WORLD CUP

The FIFA World Cup is a month-long celebration of football which is held every four years. Teams from 32 countries battle it out on the pitch for the ultimate prize in football – the World Cup trophy.

Winning the World Cup is the crowning moment of any football player's career.

## GREAT PLAYERS

What makes a great World Cup player? Some stars will always stand out. Brazil's Pelé dominated the 1970 World Cup. It was the first time a World Cup had been seen on colour TV and Brazil's football seemed as bright as their yellow shirts. Diego Maradona propelled Argentina to World Cup glory in 1986 through a combination of genius and streetwise cunning. Johan Cruyff only finished with a runners-up medal in 1974, but gave his name to the 'Cruyff turn' and treated the world to the first display of 'total football'.

## GREAT GOALS

Goalscorers win tournaments, which is why Brazil's Ronaldo makes the top ten, as does Germany's Jürgen Klinsmann, who scored three or more goals in three successive tournaments. But there are other considerations to be made in selecting the greatest World Cup players. Creative genius sees Zinedine Zidane and Andrés Iniesta in the top rank. Sometimes the victorious team's most important player is a defender, or their goalkeeper, which is why Germany's Manuel Neuer is included.

## WORLD CUP FAST FACTS

**FOUNDED:** 1930

**NUMBER OF TEAMS THAT TAKE PART:** 32 (expanded from 16 in 1978 and again from 24 in 1982)

**MOST SUCCESSFUL TEAM:** Brazil

**TOP GOAL-SCORER:** Miroslav Klose (16)

**FORMAT:** For the group stage, teams are put in eight groups of four teams. Each team plays all the other three teams once. The top two teams from each group qualify for the knockout stages, where the winner of one group plays the runner-up of another. The winners of this qualify for the eight-team quarter-finals, which are followed by the semi-finals and the long-awaited World Cup final itself.

## LEADERS

Leadership is vital for every side, and Bobby Moore inspired his men through his unflappable approach. He was an immaculate defender, but also managed to make two goals for England in the 1966 World Cup final. Age is also a factor and to win the World Cup at 40, as Italy's goalkeeper and captain Dino Zoff did, is a fantastic achievement.

## UP FOR DEBATE

This selection will always be controversial. Players who can count themselves unlucky not to make the top ten include Hungary's star of 1954, Ferenc Puskás, West Germany's heroes of 1974, Franz Beckenbauer and Gerd Müller, and England's 1966 hat-trick legend Geoff Hurst. But hopefully readers will agree on one thing, all ten players in this book have, in many different ways, contributed to the magic of the World Cup.

Pelé's amazing skills lit up four World Cup tournaments.

BOBBY MOORE

This statue of Bobby Moore, one of England's greatest ever players, stands outside Wembley Stadium in London.

# BOBBY MOORE

**FAST FACTS**

**DATE OF BIRTH:** 12 April 1941 [died 24 February 1993]

**PLACE OF BIRTH:** Barking

**COUNTRY REPRESENTED:** England

**POSITION:** Central defender

**WORLD CUPS PLAYED IN:** 1962, 1966, 1970

**CLUBS PLAYED FOR:** West Ham, Fulham, San Antonio Thunder, Seattle Sounders, Herning Fremad

*'My captain, my leader, my right-hand man. He was the spirit and the heartbeat of the team.'*

**Sir Alf Ramsey, England manager**

**Bobby Moore is the only England captain ever to lift the World Cup. He was a superb defender who relied on timing rather than strength, reading the game brilliantly and often intercepting the ball before he needed to tackle.**

## GOAL MAGIC

Moore played in the 1962 World Cup in Chile, and in all six games of England's 1966 World Cup triumph. He made England's first goal in the World Cup final against West Germany with a chipped free kick to his West Ham teammate Geoff Hurst, who headed the ball powerfully into the goal. Moore also made England's fourth and decisive goal in the last minute of extra-time with a beautiful long ball out of defence to Hurst, who crashed the ball into the top corner of the net. The image of the clean-cut, blond-haired Moore lifting the Jules Rimet trophy entered English folklore.

## TESTING TIMES

Moore's cool, unflappable image was tested in the 1970 World Cup in Mexico. He was accused of stealing a bracelet from a jewellery shop in Bogotá, Colombia, arrested by police and placed under house arrest for four days, before all charges were dropped. Moore went on to play in all England's games and gave a superb performance in the 1–0 group game defeat by Brazil. His precisely timed challenge on the powerful winger Jairzinho was hailed as the perfect tackle, and the Brazilian football legend Pelé (see pages 8–9) described Moore as the best defender he had ever played against.

## NATIONAL HERO

Moore played his last international match in 1973, having won a then record 108 caps for his country. When Moore died of cancer in 1993 there was a national outpouring of grief and thousands of scarves were placed in a shrine at the gates of his old club West Ham United. A statue of Moore now stands outside Wembley Stadium (see page 5).

Bobby Moore and Pelé swapped shirts at the end of their group match to show their mutual respect.

### DID YOU KNOW?

Moore almost didn't play in the 1966 World Cup because he was out of contract at West Ham and technically ineligible. Only the intervention of manager Sir Alf Ramsey persuaded him to sign a contract on the eve of the tournament.

> 'Before the match, I told myself that Pelé was just flesh and bones like the rest of us. Later I realised I'd been wrong.'
>
> *Tarcisio Burgnich,*
> *Italy defender*

# Pelé

**FAST FACTS**

**DATE OF BIRTH:**
23 October 1940

**PLACE OF BIRTH:**
Três Corações

**COUNTRY REPRESENTED:** Brazil

**POSITION:** Striker

**WORLD CUPS PLAYED IN:** 1958, 1962, 1966, 1970

**CLUBS PLAYED FOR:** Santos, New York Cosmos

**Edson Arantes do Nascimento, better known as Pelé, was the brightest star in a Brazil team packed full of talent and flair.**

## EARLY SUCCESS

Pelé made his international debut at just 16, and in 1958 at 17 years and 249 days old he was the then youngest player to play in a World Cup (Northern Ireland's Norman Whiteside later broke his record). He scored a hat trick in the semi-final win over France and two goals in the 1958 World Cup final – a brilliant 5–2 victory against Sweden – including a superb chip over a defender and a volley into the net. After scoring in the first match of the 1962 World Cup, Pelé was injured and missed Brazil's victory.

## WORLD CLASS

Pelé will always be best remembered for his brilliant performances for Brazil at the 1970 World Cup. He scored with a header in the final against Italy and made the decisive pass for Brazil's fourth goal scored by Carlos Alberto in a memorable 4–1 victory. This final goal was the result of wonderful passing by Brazil, with eight players involved in the move, and is often described as the greatest goal in World Cup history. Pelé scored a total of four goals in the tournament, nearly netted from the halfway line against Czechoslovakia and inspired England's goalkeeper Gordon Banks to make the best save of his career.

## GREATEST TEAM

Pelé became the first player to score in three successive World Cups in 1966, but threatened never to play in a World Cup again after being injured by tough tackling as Brazil failed to qualify from the group stage. Thankfully he went back on his threat in 1970, and became the talisman for the creative flair and 'Samba football' of Brazil's greatest side. For many people, he is the greatest player of all time.

### DID YOU KNOW?

Pelé had a part in the 1981 film 'Escape To Victory' along with Bobby Moore, Sylvester Stallone and Michael Caine. He plays a prisoner in a World War Two camp who escapes during an exhibition football match against Germany.

Pelé was an unbelievable talent on the pitch, forcing the opposition into fouls and clumsy tackles.

*'We showed the world you could enjoy being a footballer, you could laugh and have a fantastic time. I represent the era which proved that attractive football was enjoyable and successful.'*

Johan Cruyff

# Johan Cruyff

Johan Cruyff was a striker, but could pop up anywhere on the pitch. His ball skills were mesmerising and he invented 'the Cruyff turn' against Sweden, a feint and drag back that left defenders floundering.

The Netherlands team line up to sing their national anthem before the World Cup final.

**FAST FACTS**

**DATE OF BIRTH:** 25 April 1947 [died 24 March 2016]

**PLACE OF BIRTH:** Amsterdam

**COUNTRY REPRESENTED:** Netherlands

**POSITION:** Striker/attacking midfielder

**WORLD CUPS PLAYED IN:** 1974

**CLUBS PLAYED FOR:** Ajax, Barcelona, Los Angeles Aztecs, Washington Diplomats, Levante, Ajax, Feyenoord

## TOTAL FOOTBALL

At the 1974 World Cup Cruyff was the chief conductor of a great Netherlands side and its brand of 'total football'. World football had never seen anything like it as the Dutch players exchanged positions in a flexible system that baffled opponents.

## QUALIFYING WITH EASE

The Netherlands began the 1974 World Cup tournament in style, with Cruyff scoring twice in a 4-0 demolition of Argentina. His first goal saw a typical piece of instant control before he rounded the goalkeeper. Cruyff was again the star of a great 2-0 win against Brazil in a crucial second round victory. He scored the second goal with a memorable flying volley after another brilliant Dutch move.

## CUP UPSET

The Netherlands' opening goal in the 1974 World Cup final against West Germany followed a flowing passing move. Cruyff ran from near the halfway line into the penalty box and was brought down by German midfielder Hoeness. Cruyff's teammate Neeskens converted the penalty. But the Dutch reckoned without the fighting spirit of West Germany, who went on to win the final 2-1, with Gerd Müller getting the deciding goal. Yet it was the total football of Cruyff's Dutch team that most people remembered from 1974.

## RETIREMENT

Sadly Cruyff retired from international football just before the 1978 World Cup tournament, following a kidnap threat to his family. But he will be forever remembered as the number 14 in brilliant orange who lit up the 1974 World Cup.

## DID YOU KNOW?

Johan Cruyff's son Jordi played for Manchester United from 1996 to 2000, making 34 league appearances and scoring eight goals.

# DINO ZOFF

**FAST FACTS**

**DATE OF BIRTH:** 28 February 1942

**PLACE OF BIRTH:** Mariano del Friuli

**COUNTRY REPRESENTED:** Italy

**POSITION:** Goalkeeper

**WORLD CUPS PLAYED IN:** 1974, 1978, 1982

**CLUBS PLAYED FOR:** Udinese, Mantova, Napoli, Juventus

Dino Zoff is the oldest player ever to win a World Cup. The legendary Italian goalkeeper was 40 years, four months and 13 days old when he captained Italy to a 3–1 victory against West Germany in the 1982 World Cup final.

## GREAT GOALIE

Zoff was an imposing figure. At 1.8 metres, he wasn't tall for a goalkeeper, but he more than made up for it with his athleticism and huge hands. He made superb reaction saves and was an intimidating presence in a one-on-one situation. His air of calm inspired the resolute Italian defence.

## WAITING GAME

Zoff was in the squad for the 1970 Mexico World Cup, but had to be content with a reserve role. By 1974 he was the first choice goalkeeper and played in all three group games as Italy went out of the tournament on goal difference. It was in the first group game that Haiti ended Zoff's astonishing record of 1,142 minutes without conceding a goal for Italy. At the 1978 World Cup Zoff was named team captain, a rare honour for a goalkeeper. He kept a clean sheet as Italy beat the eventual winners Argentina in the group stage and was unlucky to see his side miss out on the final after losing to the Netherlands. He was criticised for letting in Arie Haan's long-range shot and some said his reflexes were slowing.

## GLORY AT LAST

But the 1982 World Cup was to belong to Zoff, the man nicknamed 'The Monument of Italian Football'. He kept another clean sheet in the semi-final win against Poland, and, in the second round game against Brazil, produced a great late save from Oscar's header as Italy beat the tournament favourites 3–2. He produced another crucial block while Italy were one goal up in the final against West Germany. The Italians went on to win the final 3–1. The sight of a 40-year-old in a goalkeeper's jersey lifting the World Cup trophy is one of the greatest World Cup moments.

*'Dino was Italy's most important player in 1982. He was the one who truly represented the team. He was an example to all of us, myself more than anyone.'*

*Paolo Rossi, Italy striker*

Dino Zoff proudly displays the World Cup trophy to the crowd and press.

### DID YOU KNOW?

Zoff came from a family of farmers. He joked: 'If I weren't a goalkeeper I couldn't be anything else but a farmer with the hands I've got.'

*'It was like pick–pocketing the English and stealing a win.'*
**Maradona**

# DIEGO MARADONA

**FAST FACTS**

**DATE OF BIRTH:** 30 October 1960

**PLACE OF BIRTH:** Lanús, Buenos Aires

**COUNTRY REPRESENTED:** Argentina

**POSITION:** Attacking midfielder, second striker

**WORLD CUPS PLAYED IN:** 1982, 1986, 1990, 1994

**CLUBS PLAYED FOR:** Argentinos Juniors, Boca Juniors, Barcelona, Napoli, Sevilla, Newell's Old Boys

Diego Maradona was a tremendously skilful forward for Argentina, who grew up in poverty in Buenos Aires. With his low centre of gravity and superb dribbling and passing, Maradona was considered to be the best player in the world in the 1980s.

### HAND OF GOD

Always controversial, Maradona scored twice in the 1982 World Cup, but was sent off against Brazil. He is best remembered for the contrasting goals he scored against England in the 1986 World Cup quarter-final in Mexico. For his first, he punched the ball over England's goalkeeper Peter Shilton. The referee believed Maradona had headed the ball and the goal stood. Maradona later said the goal was 'a little with the head of Maradona and a little with the Hand of God'. The expression stuck.

### GENIUS GOALS

Maradona's second goal was one of the best individual goals ever seen as he sprinted from his own half, taking 11 touches and beating five England players before rounding Shilton to score. It is often described as the goal of the century. In the semi-final, a 3–2 win against Belgium, Maradona scored twice, including another superb solo effort. In the final against West Germany he laid on the pass for the winning goal in a thrilling 3–2 victory. The

genius of Maradona had propelled an average Argentina team to World Cup glory.

### TROUBLED TIMES

Despite being hampered by an ankle injury during the 1990 World Cup, Maradona still set up the goal that helped Argentina reach the final, where they lost to a late goal by West Germany's Andreas Brehme. Maradona was in tears at the final whistle.

### THE END

By the 1994 World Cup Maradona's lifestyle was increasingly chaotic. He played twice in the 1994 World Cup, scoring a memorable goal against Greece and running to the camera with a wild-eyed stare. After the match he tested positive for using ephedrine, a performance-enhancing drug. Maradona was never to play international football again as his incredible career of 91 games and 34 goals ended in disgrace.

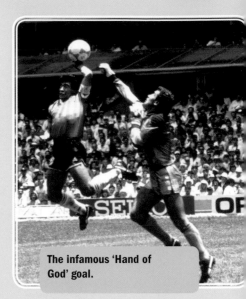

The infamous 'Hand of God' goal.

### DID YOU KNOW?

As a child Maradona fell into a pit of sewage and nearly drowned before being saved by his Uncle Cirilo.

Maradona sprints to celebrate with his teammates after scoring against Greece at the 1994 World Cup.

*'We can only win by giving everything and being ready to defeat the adversary with fiery aggression.'*

*Jürgen Klinsmann*

# Jürgen Klinsmann

**FAST FACTS**

**DATE OF BIRTH:** 30 July 1964

**PLACE OF BIRTH:** Göppingen

**COUNTRY REPRESENTED:** West Germany, Germany

**POSITION:** Striker

**WORLD CUPS PLAYED IN:** 1990, 1994, 1998

**CLUBS PLAYED FOR:** VfB Stuttgart, Inter Milan, Monaco, Tottenham Hotspur, Bayern Munich, Sampdoria, Orange County Blue Star

Jürgen Klinsmann was one of Germany's greatest ever marksmen. The blond striker scored 11 goals in 17 World Cup games and was the first player to score three goals or more in three successive World Cups.

## FANTASTIC FINISHER

Klinsmann was superb at getting in front of his marker and could finish with diving headers, volleys and precise shots. The highlight of his career was winning the 1990 World Cup with West Germany. He scored three goals in the tournament, including a typical near-post finish for the vital first goal against the Netherlands in the last-16 round, a great flicked header against Yugoslavia and another header versus the United Arab Emirates in the group games.

## QUICK EXIT

Klinsmann scored five times at the 1994 World Cup for the reunified Germany side, even though Germany unexpectedly lost to Bulgaria in the quarter-final. Possibly the best goal of his career was his flick-up and turn for a stunning volley against South Korea.

## CAPTAIN KLINSMANN

Although the German side was ageing in the 1998 World Cup, Klinsmann as captain again showed his class with three very different goals: showing great control before volleying home against the USA, scoring with a diving header after the ball rebounded off the post against Iran, and a poached effort against Mexico. He went on to manage an acclaimed Germany team at the 2006 World Cup andreached the last-16 as head coach of the USA at the 2014 World Cup.

## DID YOU KNOW?

When Klinsmann made his debut for Tottenham Hotspur in 1994, he celebrated scoring at Sheffield Wednesday by making an exaggerated dive to mock claims that he went down too easily when tackled.

Klinsmann is tackled by Igor Štimac of Croatia during their 1998 quarter-final clash.

*'To hold the World Cup in my hands is one of the most incredible moments of my life.'*

*Ronaldo*

# RONALDO

**Brazil's Ronaldo was said to be the world's most complete striker — a fantastic dribbler and instinctive finisher who scored a magnificent 15 goals in World Cup tournaments.**

## FINAL HEARTBREAK

When Brazil reached the 1998 World Cup final in Paris, Ronaldo had already scored four times, including a great effort off the outside of his boot against Morocco and Brazil's goal in the 1–1 draw with the Netherlands in the semi-final. He also converted the vital first penalty in the semi-final shoot-out win. But the world was stunned when Ronaldo suffered a mysterious fit on the eve of the final and was first left off the Brazil team sheet, then reinstated just half an hour before kick-off. He was clearly not fit to play the match and France went on to win 3–0.

## GOAL MACHINE

Ronaldo erased that unhappy memory by scoring both Brazil's goals in the 2002 World Cup final against Germany. That big smile returned as he first pounced on a rebound off Oliver Kahn the German keeper, then produced a precise finish from the edge of the box. He scored eight goals in the tournament and won the Golden Boot as top scorer. His tally included a goal from a seemingly impossible angle against Costa Rica and a lovely shot with the outside of his right boot to win the semi-final against Turkey.

## FITNESS AND FORM

Ronaldo scored a hat–trick of penalties against Argentina in a qualifying match for the 2006 World Cup, but was criticised by some for being overweight at the tournament. He still scored twice against Japan and once against Ghana, his 15th World Cup goal featuring a typically nonchalant dummy to round the goalkeeper and score.

Ronaldo does his trademark finger-wagging celebration after scoring the first goal in the 2002 World Cup final.

**FAST FACTS**

**DATE OF BIRTH:** 22 September 1976

**PLACE OF BIRTH:** Rio de Janeiro

**COUNTRY REPRESENTED:** Brazil

**POSITION:** Striker

**WORLD CUPS PLAYED IN:** 1998, 2002, 2006

**CLUBS PLAYED FOR:** Cruzeiro, PSV Eindhoven, Barcelona, Inter Milan, Real Madrid, AC Milan, Corinthians

# ZINEDINE ZIDANE

**Zinedine Zidane was a magician of a midfielder. He could find space and make passes from seemingly impossible angles.**

### FRENCH HERO

Born to French Algerian parents in Marseille, Zidane opted to play for France and did much to promote racial unity in the country. In the 1998 World Cup, his two headed goals helped win the final for France as they beat Brazil 3–0 in Paris. Zidane had been instrumental in France's run to the final. He became a national hero and his image was projected onto the famous Arc de Triomphe after France won the Cup.

### MIDFIELD MAESTRO

Injury kept Zidane out of all but one of France's games at the 2002 World Cup as the holders crashed out at the group stage in a memorable tournament upset. Two years later, in 2004, Zidane announced his retirement from international football. But it was to be shortlived, as Zidane returned to Les Bleus to help inspire France to the World Cup final in 2006, setting up the winning goal against Brazil in the quarter-final and scoring the winner with a penalty against Portugal in the semi-final.

### CLOSE GAME

Having announced he was to retire once more from football after the final, most neutrals were willing on Zidane to win another World Cup winners' medal. He scored with an audacious chipped penalty after seven minutes, only for Marco Materazzi to equalise for Italy. When the game went into extra-time Zidane almost won it for France as Buffon made a brilliant save to tip over his header.

### MOMENT OF MADNESS

Then with ten minutes of extra-time left, came an astonishing moment. In an off-the-ball incident Zidane headbutted Marco Materazzi in the chest and was sent off. The world speculated what Materazzi had said to provoke such a reaction. Materazzi later admitted that he had insulted Zidane's sister. Despite the red card and France going on to lose to Italy on penalties, Zidane still received a rousing welcome home in France. If anything the incident cemented his love affair with the nation.

*'Playing for the team has given me my greatest satisfaction, my greatest joy.'*

**Zinedine Zidane, on playing for the French national team**

**DID YOU KNOW?**

After Zinedine Zidane's heroic performances for France in the 1998 World Cup, Italy coach Cesare Maldini announced: 'I would give up five players to have Zizou [Zidane] in my squad.'

**FAST FACTS**

**DATE OF BIRTH:** 23 June 1972

**PLACE OF BIRTH:** Marseille

**COUNTRY REPRESENTED:** France

**POSITION:** Attacking midfield

**WORLD CUPS PLAYED IN:** 1998, 2002, 2006

**CLUBS PLAYED FOR:** Cannes, Bordeaux, Juventus, Real Madrid

> 'I don't play the game to be number one. I play to be happy.'

# ANDRÉS INIESTA

Andrés Iniesta is the mastermind behind the 'tiki taka' passing game of Spain. His game relies upon superb balance, his feel for the ball, quick feet and a tremendous range of flicks and feints.

## DID YOU KNOW?

Iniesta keeps every pair of boots that he has played in, including his first boots, a pair of size eight Adidas Predators.

Iniesta scores an extraordinary extra-time goal in the 2010 World Cup Final.

**FAST FACTS**

**DATE OF BIRTH:** 11 May 1984

**PLACE OF BIRTH:** Fuentealbilla

**COUNTRY REPRESENTED:** Spain

**POSITION:** Attacking midfielder

**WORLD CUPS PLAYED IN:** 2006, 2010

**CLUBS PLAYED FOR:** Barcelona

## MIDFIELD MASTER

Iniesta played at the heart of the most successful Spanish national team of all time, forming an instinctive partnership with midfielder Xavi. Although he is a relatively slight figure, Iniesta is very difficult to take the ball off once he goes on a dribble.

## WORLD CUP WIZARD

Iniesta was in the Spain squad for the 2006 World Cup, playing just once before they were knocked out of the tournament 3–1 by France in the second round. However, the highlight of Iniesta's career so far has undoubtedly been scoring the winning goal for Spain in the 2010 World Cup Final against the Netherlands in Johannesburg. He scored in the 116th minute, four minutes from the end of extra-time, just as a penalty shoot-out appeared inevitable. Found by Barcelona teammate Cesc Fabregas on the edge of the box, Iniesta waited for the ball to drop before sending an expert half-volley past the Dutch goalkeeper, Stekelenburg. He whipped off his shirt, revealing a white vest with a tribute to Dani Jarque, a former youth player who died of a heart attack in 2009. Iniesta was named man of the match in the final.

Match-winner Iniesta grabs the trophy as Spain wins the World Cup for the first time.

## SPANISH SKILLS

What makes Iniesta almost the complete footballer is his ability to play anywhere, though his best position is as an attacking midfielder. A product of Barcelona's youth system and a modest man off the pitch, Iniesta completed a tremendous international treble through winning not only the 2010 World Cup, but also the 2008 and 2012 European Championships with Spain.

'A lot has changed for Germany since 2010. Back then it was not certain tha_ I would be the number one. Now I'm glad about the responsibility I take for the team.'

*Manuel Neuer*

# Manuel Neuer

**Manuel Neuer is considered to be the best goalkeeper in the world and one of the most talented shot-stoppers in the history of the sport. Neuer was the foundation for Germany's victory at the 2014 World Cup.**

**FAST FACTS**

**DATE OF BIRTH:** 27 March 1986

**PLACE OF BIRTH:** Gelsenkirchen

**COUNTRY REPRESENTED:** Germany

**POSITION:** Goalkeeper

**WORLD CUPS PLAYED IN:** 2010, 2014

**CLUBS PLAYED FOR:** Schalke, Bayern Munich

**DID YOU KNOW?**

Neuer did the voiceover for Disney character Frank McCay in the German version of the 2013 animation Monsters University.

## A COMPLETE KEEPER

Neuer has all the attributes it takes to be one of the all-time greats. His speed, reflexes and agility, combined with his strength and size allow Neuer to make sensational saves. Neuer is a commanding presence who organises his side's defence and dominates his penalty area. He is a master at rushing quickly off his line to thwart strikers and catch crosses.

## AN ELEVENTH MAN

What really sets Neuer apart is his ability to play the ball out from the back. He is a strong thrower and has excellent ball control and footwork. Neuer is perfectly confident in coming out of his area to play the ball. Due to his style of play, experts have dubbed him as a 'sweeper keeper'. For his team, it is like playing with 11 outfield players.

## WORLD CUP CALL-UP

Neuer was selected as Germany's number one at the 2010 World Cup. During the group stages he only conceded one goal. In the 4-1 second round victory over England, Neuer turned provider, setting up one of the goals for Miroslav Klose. Another clean sheet in the 4-0 drubbing of Argentina was followed by a narrow 1-0 semi-final defeat to Spain.

## THE GOLDEN GLOVE

Neuer was instrumental in his side's World Cup victory in 2014. His 'sweeper keeper' playing style and outfield roaming allowed his teammates to press the opponents in their own half. In the quarter-final Neuer kept his third clean sheet of the tournament in a 1-0 defeat of France. A late goal was conceded in the 7-1 semi-final demolition of Brazil but it hardly mattered. In the final Neuer was supreme again, commanding his area well and not even letting Argentina have a shot on target. Afterwards Neuer was awarded with the Golden Glove which crowned him the tournament's best goalkeeper.

# STARS OF THE FUTURE

Football is always looking out for the next Pelé or Maradona, especially at World Cup tournaments. Here are just a few players who may light up the World Cup in the future.

## NEYMAR (BRAZIL)

Tagged 'the next Pelé' by some, the Brazil striker has huge potential and scored more than a hundred goals at Santos before joining Barcelona. At the age of just 24 he scored his 50th goal for Brazil. A great dribbler and finisher, Neymar can score both short and long-range goals. His flicks, backheels, stepovers and choreographed celebrations (plus his sometimes Mohican hairstyle and an earring) will surely enliven the World Cup for years to come.

## HARRY KANE (ENGLAND)

If England are going to win a World Cup in the near future, Harry Kane is the man most likely to score them the goals. The Tottenham Hostpur striker has that special ability to find the back of the net. Kane can score goals inside and outside the box with a cracking shot that possesses both power and accuracy.

## PAUL POGBA (FRANCE)

French central midfielder Paul Pogba became the most expensive footballer on the planet when he was signed by Manchester United. Pogba has everything it takes to be a World Cup star. He is tall, powerful and strong, yet he has skills, flair and creativity in abundance too. Pogba's explosive style can turn defence into attack in a flash.

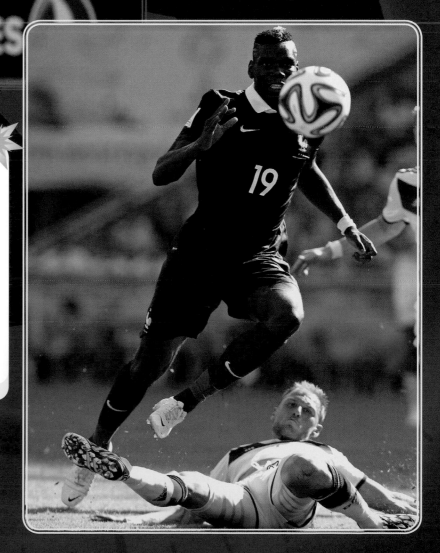

# WORLD CUP

**1.** Bobby Moore, the captain of England's 1966 World Cup-winning side played for which English side?

a) Manchester United
b) Liverpool
c) West Ham United

**2.** After his two goals helped France win the 1998 World Cup, the image of Zinedine Zidane was projected onto what iconic French structure?

a) The Eiffel Tower
b) The Arc de Triomphe
c) Notre Dame

**3.)** Whom did Maradona score his 'Hand of God' goal against in 1986?

a) Belgium
b) West Germany
c) England

**4.** How old was Italy goalkeeper Dino Zoff when he picked up the 1982 World Cup?

a) 40
b) 41
c) 39

**5.** What award did Germany's Manuel Neuer win at the 2014 World Cup?

a) Golden Ball
b) Golden Glove
c) Golden Boot

**6.** Johan Cruyff lent his name to 'the Cruyff turn' after a dummy against which side in the 1974 World Cup?

a) West Germany
b) Argentina
c) Sweden

**7.** What happened to Brazil's Ronaldo on the eve of the 1998 World Cup final?

a) He suffered a groin strain
b) He broke his metatarsal bone
c) He suffered a fit

**8.** Pelé made the decisive pass for Brazil's fourth goal in the 1970 World Cup final. Who scored it?

a) Jairzinho
b) Carlos Alberto
c) Rivelino

**9.** Who was the goalkeeper that Maradona rounded when scoring 'the goal of the century' in the 1986 World Cup?

a) Peter Shilton
b) Harald Schumacher
c) Ray Clemence

**10.** Which English team did German striker Jürgen Klinsmann once play for?

a) Arsenal
b) Tottenham Hotspur
c) Manchester City

# EXPERT QUIZ

**11. When Andrés Iniesta scored the winner for Spain in the 2010 World Cup final, he revealed a vest with a slogan. Was it?**

a) An advertisement for a Spanish bank
b) A tribute to a Spanish youth player who had died
c) A message thanking God

**12. When Zinedine Zidane was sent off in the 2006 World Cup final, was it for?**

a) Pushing the referee
b) Biting an opponent
c) Headbutting an opponent

**13. In the 1966 World Cup final Bobby Moore's long pass released which player to score England's fourth goal?**
a) Geoff Hurst
b) Roger Hunt
c) Martin Peters

**14. Johan Cruyff helped create a particular style of football for the Netherlands in 1974. Was it?**

a) Total football
b) Tiki taka
c) Route one

**15. How old was Pelé when he made his international debut?**

a) 18
b) 17
c) 16

**16. How many goals did Brazil's Ronaldo score in the 2002 World Cup?**

a) Six
b) Eight
c) Seven

**17. How many clean sheets did Germany's Manuel Neuer keep in the 2014 World Cup?**

a) Three
b) Four
c) Five

**18. Argentina's Maradona made the winning goal against West Germany in the 1986 World Cup final. But who scored it?**

a) Brown
b) Burruchaga
c) Valdano

**19. Bobby Moore was said to have made the perfect tackle against Brazil in the 1970 World Cup. Who was it he tackled?**

a) Pelé
b) Gerson
c) Jairzinho

**20. Spain's Iniesta scored the winner in the 2010 World Cup final against the Netherlands. In what city was the game played?**

a) Johannesburg
b) Cape Town
c) Pretoria

**Answers:** 1) c 2) b 3) c 4) d 5) b 6) b 7) c 8) b 9) a 10) b 11) b 12) c 13) b 14) a 15) c 16) b 17) b 18) b 19) b 20) a

# GLOSSARY

**Ball:** Another word for a pass, i.e. a long ball, short ball, etc.

**Cap:** When you award someone a cap in football, you pick them to play for their country.

**Central defender:** Someone who plays in the middle of the defence, defending the goal area directly in front of the goalkeeper.

**Chip:** A pass or shot that is kicked high up in the air, but then descends to its intended target.

**Clean sheet:** Not conceding any goals.

**Cruyff turn:** A move made popular by Johan Cruyff in 1974. It involves a dummy and drag back of the ball that deceives a defender.

**Debut:** A player's first appearance is known as making a debut.

**Diving header:** A header that is made while diving full length to reach the ball.

**Extra-time:** A period of 30 extra minutes that is played if a knockout game is a draw at the end of the standard 90 minutes.

**Feint:** Where a player uses their body to look as if they are going one way, but then go another.

**Fit:** A sudden violent attack that can be accompanied by convulsions and may make you fall unconscious.

**Free kick:** This is awarded when a player is fouled. The fouled team is given a free kick at the ball with no opposition player allowed within ten yards (9.1 metres) of them.

**Half-volley:** A shot taken when the ball has bounced once.

**Hat-trick:** When a player scores three goals it is said to be a hat-trick.

**Intercept:** This involves anticipating a pass by the opposition and taking the ball before it reaches its intended target.

**Neutral:** Someone who doesn't support either of the two teams playing.

**Outfield player:** Any player who is not a goalkeeper.

**Overhead kick:** Kicking a high ball over the back of your head with both legs off the ground and one leg higher than the other in a kind of 'scissor' movement. Also known as a bicycle kick.

**Performance-enhancing:** A drug that improves a player's performance is known as performance–enhancing.

**Reaction save:** A save relying on the quick reflexes of the goalkeeper.

**Striker:** A forward who plays close to the opposition goal and whose main purpose is to score goals.

**Sweeper:** A defender who 'sweeps' up the danger, playing behind one or two centre backs. The sweeper can also move forward when there is the chance to attack.

**Talisman:** A player of vital importance to a side, who also brings luck and confidence to the other players.

**Tiki taka:** The short-passing style of play made famous by the Spain football team.

**Total football:** A fluid style of play created by the Netherlands side of 1974, involving players skilful enough to swap positions.

**Volley:** A shot taken when the ball is off the ground.

**Youth system:** A training school for young players, usually attached to a particular football club.

# WORLD CUP WINNERS TABLE

| Year | Winners | Final score | Runners-up | Venue | Location |
|------|---------|-------------|------------|-------|----------|
| 1930 | Uruguay | 4-2 | Argentina | Estadio Centenario | Montevideo, Uruguay |
| 1934 | Italy | 2-1 | Czechoslovakia | Stadio Nazionale PNF | Rome, Italy |
| 1938 | Italy | 4-2 | Hungary | Stade Olympique de Colombes | Paris, France |
| 1950 | Uruguay | 2-1 | Brazil | Estádio do Maracanã | Rio de Janeiro, Brazil |
| 1954 | West Germany | 3-2 | Hungary | Wankdorf Stadium | Bern, Switzerland |
| 1958 | Brazil | 5-2 | Sweden | Råsunda Stadium | Solna, Sweden |
| 1962 | Brazil | 3-1 | Czechoslovakia | Estadio Nacional | Santiago, Chile |
| 1966 | England | 4-2 | West Germany | Wembley Stadium | London, England |
| 1970 | Brazil | 4-1 | Italy | Estadio Azteca | Mexico City, Mexico |
| 1974 | West Germany | 2-1 | Netherlands | Olympiastadio | Munich, West Germany |
| 1978 | Argentina | 3-1 | Netherlands | Estadio Monumental | Buenos Aires, Argentina |
| 1982 | Italy | 3-1 | West Germany | Santiago Bernabéu | Madrid, Spain |
| 1986 | Argentina | 3-2 | West Germany | Estadio Azteca | Mexico City, Mexico |
| 1990 | West Germany | 1-0 | Argentina | Stadio Olimpico | Rome, Italy |
| 1994 | Brazil | 0-0 (3-2 on penalties) | Italy | Rose Bowl | Pasadena, California, USA |
| 1998 | France | 3-0 | Brazil | Stade de France | Saint-Denis, France |
| 2002 | Brazil | 2-0 | Germany | International Stadium | Yokohama, Japan |
| 2006 | Italy | 1-1 (5-3 on penalties) | France | Olympiastadion | Berlin, Germany |
| 2010 | Spain | 1-0 | Netherlands | Soccer City | Johannesburg, South Africa |
| 2014 | Germany | 1-0 | Argentina | Estádio do Maracanã | Rio de Janeiro, Brazil |

# FURTHER INFORMATION

## WEB LINKS

http://www.bbc.co.uk/sport/0/football/21317369
Watch Bobby Moore's 'perfect tackle' on Jairzinho (1970)

http://www.youtube.com/watch?v=OHrjevD2vhk
Brazil's wonderful team goal (1970)

http://www.youtube.com/watch?v=U1k7DGqRF5g
The famous Cruyff turn (1974)

http://www.youtube.com/watch?v=ATfjrnet_Dk
Klinsmann's goal against South Korea (1994)

http://news.bbc.co.uk/sport1/hi/football/world_cup_2010/8808966.stm
Iniesta wins the World Cup (2010)

## BOOKS

**Foul Football: Wicked World Cup**, Michael Coleman (Scholastic, 2010)
**Inside Sport: World Cup Football**, Clive Gifford (Wayland, 2010)
**The World Cup: World Cup 2010**, Michael Hurley (Heinemann, 2010)

# INDEX